Library of
Davidson College

Series / Number 90-008

Inner Dualism: *An Outcome of the Center-Periphery Relationship During Modernization Processes in Uganda*

BARUCH KIMMERLING
MOSHE LISSAK

The Hebrew University, Jerusalem

SAGE PUBLICATIONS / Beverly Hills / London

Copyright © 1973 by Sage Publications, Inc.

Printed in the United States of America

All rights reserved. No part of this book may be reproduced or utilized in any form or by any means, electronic or mechanical, including photocopying, recording, or by any information storage and retrieval system, without permission in writing from the publisher.

338.1
K49i

For information address:

SAGE PUBLICATIONS, INC.
275 South Beverly Drive
Beverly Hills, California 90212

SAGE PUBLICATIONS, INC.
St George's House / 44 Hatton Garden
London EC1N 8ER

International Standard Book Number 0-8039-0366-9

Library of Congress Catalog Card No. 73-92222

FIRST PRINTING

When citing a Research Paper, please use the proper form. Remember to cite the series title and include the paper number. One of the two following formats can be adapted (depending on the style manual used):

(1) WEINTRAUB, D. (1973) "Development and Modernization in the Philippines: The Problem of Change in the Context of Political Stability and Social Continuity." Sage Research Papers in the Social Sciences (Studies in Comparative Modernization Series, No. 90-001). Beverly Hills and London: Sage Publications.

or

75-10190

(2) Weintraub, Dov. 1973. *Development and Modernization in the Philippines: The Problem of Change in the Context of Political Stability and Social Continuity.* Sage Research Papers in the Social Sciences, vol. 1, series no. 90-001 (Studies in Comparative Modernization Series). Beverly Hills and London: Sage Publications.

Contents

Editor's Introduction to the Series *5*

Introduction *7*

Toward Crystallization of a Unitary State *10*

The Agrarian Policies of the Centers *18*

Inner-Dualism—A Response of the Periphery *22*

The Extension of the Inner Dualistic Pattern *28*

Conclusions *32*

Notes *34*

References *38*

Editor's Introduction to the Series

This series of comparative studies on modernization stems from a broad programme of research developed over the past five years in the Harry S Truman Research Institute, in cooperation with the Department of Sociology of the Hebrew University of Jerusalem, and with other departments of the Faculty of Social Sciences. Its focus is analytical and comparative—i.e., the analysis of the *diverse* social, economical and political patterns which develop in different modernizing societies and the factors which can explain such diversity.

Even though this series of papers shows considerable differences in points of view, nevertheless they have some strong common grounds; mainly, in their revision of 'classical' theories of modernization. These theories assumed that there existed a total dichotomy between 'traditional' and 'modern' societies, and that the best way for a society to modernize was to shed most of its traditional qualities.

However, the present studies support the view that the variability of modernization is not due to one factor (the traditionality of a society, or its level of development) but to a variety of factors. Neither do their authors assume that there is necessarily any negative relationship between tradition and modernity. Rather, different aspects of 'tradition' will have varying impact on the process of development, so that each society may create its own version of modernity.

So we may say of much of this research that it:

First, recognizes what may be called the systemic viability of the so-called transitional systems;

Second, assumes these societies may develop in ways not necessarily envisioned by the initial model of modernization;

Third, they recognize the importance of both the different aspects of historical continuity and of the international situation for shaping differing contours of development for different contemporary 'post-traditional' social orders.

The crystallization of any post-traditional society is influenced by a combination of social factors, including:

- The level of resources available for mobilization and institution-building,
- The manner in which the forces of modernity impinge on the particular society,
- The structure of the situation of change in which they are caught, and,
- The different traditions of these societies or civilizations as embodied in their 'pre-modern' socio-economic structure.

Differing combinations of these forces will influence different aspects of the contours and dynamics of the post-traditional socio-political order; each individual force will tend to have more influence on some developmental aspects than on others.

The studies which will be published in this series will test these generalizations against specific case studies, or in comparative analyses.

—*S. N. EISENSTADT*

Editors' Note:
The editors would like to express their gratitude to the Founders and Overseers of the Harry S Truman Research Institute for their support and assistance in the development of this series.
—*S.N.E. and D.W.*

INNER DUALISM:
An Outcome of the Center-Periphery
Relationship During Modernization
Processes in Uganda

BARUCH KIMMERLING and
MOSHE LISSAK

The Hebrew University, Jerusalem

Introduction

It is not very surprising that at the beginning of Edward Shils' (1961: 117) well known article, "Center and Periphery," he stated that "the principle of the Counter-Reformation, *Cuius regio, ejus religio,* although its rigor has been loosened and its harshness mollified, retains a core of permanent truth."[1] The meaning of this "permanent truth" seems to be the explicit or implicit belief in the potential omnipotency of the political ruling strata and their allies or satellites, which represent the instutionalized symbols and values—i.e., the center—toward its periphery.[2] Shils is not alone in his tendency to see the periphery as an object of the center's manipulation, a manipulation carried out with different degrees of effectiveness. Many other theoreticians in the social sciences,[3] in spite of their occasionally very sophisticated conception of center-periphery (or other similar terms) relationships, imply in their works that one or another structure or content of the center (e.g., democratic parliamentary leadership, paternal dictatorship, modernizing autocracy, and so forth) can be adjusted with more or less success to a certain society.

AUTHORS' NOTE: The research presented in this article is an extension of a part of a research project on Comparative Analysis Processes of Agricultural Development and Modernization, carried out under a grant of the U.S. Department of Agriculture (F.G.-IS-241), in collaboration with the Harry S. Truman Research Center.

Thanks are due to Professors S. N. Eisenstadt and D. Weintraub, who conducted the project (with the second author of this article), for helpful suggestions and comments on earlier versions of this essay. We are deeply indebted to Professor Belshaw, for his generous help given us during the visit to Uganda, and to Mrs. Gila Noam who did the editorial work.

When such an approach is applied to the field of modernization studies, the whole problem tends to be reduced to finding the most adequate and committed center, which will be able to develop the most appropriate strategies of social mobilization (Deutsch, 1961) and of the redistribution of the "defreezed" resources, assuming that "the 'masses' have responded to their contact [with the center] with a striking measure of acceptance."[4]

Our present attempt is not to remove the focus of analysis from the "center," but to emphasize also the centrality of the nature and characteristics of the "periphery" in the outcomes that are achieved from its interaction processes with the center. Without going on *ad absurdum*, we regard it fruitful for heuristic purposes to ask if it is possible—and if so, under what conditions and to what extent—for a large population to exist in a country without depending on a center as such, neither material dependence (as having a need for services, resources, or for a "law and order" supplier and coordinator), nor psychological or emotional dependence (as for establishing the existing "cognitive order" and the rules of the "distributive justice").

If we assume the possibility of the existence of such a situation, this does not necessarily imply that there are no contacts or exchange relationships between the center and "its" periphery. The center can attempt, for example, to collect taxes as well as supply roads, agricultural experts or "national ceremonies." The periphery can pay the "tributes," utilize the roads and celebrate the holiday, but along with this and despite the importance of all the items supplied by the center for "better" material and cultural survival, the periphery can remain, in the main, "intact" and self-sufficient.

As we shall see, the extent of periphery self-sufficiency in relation to the material component can be correlated with the degree of the country's development and its type. The second dimension of the periphery's self-sufficiency seems to be its ability to produce and maintain a collective identity, whose ultimate boundary is more limited than that proposed by the center.[5]

Thus, the increased emphasis on the periphery's response (or lack of response) does not exclude the need for careful examination of the center in terms of the *intensity* and *scope* of its involvement in processes of periphery "reconstruction." Intensity in this context means chiefly the extent to which the elite resorts, or threatens to resort, to force in order to insure the realization of its plans. The scope of involvement refers to the extent to which the change proposed or actually imposed upon the periphery population is a "total" one. The scope of the change is obviously narrower in the case where the proposed innovation recommends, for the most part, new techniques for soil improvements, or the introduction of new varieties of familiar crops, than in the case where the proposed reforms require *ipso facto* comprehensive organization of the production, marketing, as well as consumption systems. The contrast between the violent process of "collectivization" of the rural sector in the Soviet Union or China and conventional technical aid in many developing countries is a case in point. In the former cases, the intensity was also highest, but there is not necessarily a correlation between the intensity and the scope of the center's involvement.[6]

Analytically, it is necessary to clearly differentiate between: (a) the aims posed by the center and how it plans to carry them out, and (b) the periphery's basic reaction to the claims and the actions of the center, as well as (c) the "final" results of this interaction process—all the while taking into account the resources at the disposal of the center and peripheries.

The actions initiated by the center can come singly or as a set of complementary acts. Such a set is, for example, the frequent first stage in rural reconstruction: the introduction of the cash crops through imposition of taxes, when the "final" result can be the push of the rural sector into a monetized market system.

The periphery (or its different segments) can accept or reject— actively or passively—specific initiatives of the center, or attempt to split the offered package deal (e.g., to introduce the cash crops, but to avoid paying taxes). The various reactions of the periphery may also be classified according to their intensity and the scope of their impact upon the central political institutions. The phenomenon of sporadic violent reactions against the center, its representatives or the "order" (including the definition of the collective boundary) on the one hand, and the phenomenon of full-fledged organization directed at remolding the character of the center,[7] or changing the reallocation of resources on the other hand, are worlds apart.

The immediate as well as the cumulative spectrum of results of the interactions between the center and "its" peripheries, can be just as the center (and/or its partner-periphery) expected or planned, but sometimes can diverge very far from the expectancies of both. What seems to be a very limited act in its scope can have far-reaching consequences, crosscutting the institutional spheres, accompanied by "surprising" by-products, just as an attempt for profound changes can lead to an *ad hoc* behavioral or institutional reaction.

Our focus of attention in this essay will be the analysis of a specific case study in social change: the processes which occurred in Uganda. This is a peasant society (less than five percent of the population live in a milieu defined as "urban"), and the center/periphery dichotomy coincides with, in the main, the rural/urban one.[8] The pattern of relations between the political and economic power centers and the rural sector has a decisive impact upon the scope and the rate of modernization. This condition is implicit in Eisenstadt's statement that agricultural modernization means not only "growth of technical know-how and output, but also far-reaching structural changes in the organization of rural society and economy, such as the weakening of production for self-consumption, growth of production for the market, and the progressive weakening of closeness and self-sufficiency of rural society and its growing embodiment, through a process of specialization, in a more differentiated economy and social system."[9]

In this study we shall attempt to demonstrate such a process of interaction between the changing power-center and the rural peripheries circumscribing it—for the purpose of demonstrating that the utilization of such an analytical framework could overcome the simplicity of the one-dimensional approaches to the outcomes of the relationships between rulers and ruled.[10]

We shall analyze below the process of crystallization and building of the present Ugandan nation around its centers (colonial and post-colonial) —in addition examining the orientations of the centers toward the rural peripheries, the responses of the peripheries, and some of the institutional consequences of these relationships.

TOWARD CRYSTALLIZATION OF A UNITARY STATE

For a better understanding of the background of the complex Ugandan system and the origin of the later struggles and relations between the diverse components, we must briefly survey the political arena and its development.[11]

Uganda as an entity was built around the kingdom of Buganda which existed as an independent political system nearly 500 years before the colonial period. Buganda seems to be the natural leader and the core of the whole territory.

The various forms of mobilization and activation of political consciousness and activity were known to the inhabitants much before they could find a modern expression. Several factors combined to accelerate the rise in the level of political activity and its modernization:

Before the coming of the British there were other semi-bureaucratic political kingdoms (Bunyoro, Ankola and Toro) in the territory, besides Buganda. Although the other ethnic and tribal units were not organized as "kingdoms" and had not undergone a process of quasi-bureaucratization, they maintained a differentiated level of political activity beyond kinship-based associations.

The establishment of fairly numerous western-type educational institutions mainly in Buganda had a far-reaching influence on political activity. It resulted in the growth of educated elites of various types, from groups with a limited number of years of schooling (i.e., with only reading and writing skills) up to college graduates who had studied abroad (in comparison with other African countries, especially those not under British rule, the number of B.A.'s and doctors of medicine and law is high in Uganda). It made for familiarity with various Western ideologies, which were transferred to the Ugandan background and translated into "more familiar" terms, especially by young men who had spent several years in Europe or in the United States. This "transfer" sometimes assumed very "local" forms, especially when applied to the middle strata. Moreover, it led to an intensification of demands from the central British administration and of expectations from the local government.

There was fairly high geographical mobility, especially in the direction of the administrative and commercial center in Buganda. Thus, a fairly dense informal communication network was created beyond the local units. It promoted not only an exchange of information, opinions and goods, but also the formation and integration of various groups and organizations on different levels and for various purposes.

Foci of tensions, conflicts, struggles and conflicting interests were always present in the territory. These stemmed from various sources: economic, ethnic, religious, racial, tribal and others.[12] The multiplicity of these foci also promoted integration, since the conflicts sometimes were parallel to each other and sometimes cut across each other.

That is why there always were in Uganda relatively numerous political organizations and organizations characterized by some conspicuously political aspects. (Religious organizations, too, were aspects of the political struggle, as were also marketing cooperatives, etc.[13]).

There were two main meeting points between men from the same or from different classes in which political organizations were formed and shaped:

The first was in the various rural units: in local markets, around churches or schools (which were also missionary institutions), where men who knew each other and usually belonged to the same kinship group would meet regularly. At such "intimate" meetings, common problems were discussed, and leaders and speakers soon emerged who determined the "policies" of the neighborhood or managed "foreign relations" with the bureaucracy on all its levels and with the local government services. These leaders did not belong to the old kinship leadership (bataka), nor did they find a place in the "newer" frameworks, either bureaucratic or local-political. Their level of education was usually low; they were graduates of the missionary elementary schools. Their natural bent was towards the traditional leadership and they were usually supporters and allies of the neotraditionalistic and populistic organizations. In Buganda these meetings reached a high level of institutionalization in so-called *Miruka* units.[13]

The second focus was provided by the urban slums inhabited by Africans, particularly in Katwe near Mengo (the capital of Buganda and the court of the Kabaka), where there were numerous beer-halls in which thousands of small, unsuccessful merchants (estimated at twelve thousand in 1953) would congregate. Besides shop-talk, they would conduct "political" discussions which were mainly an expression of their antagonism towards the Asian merchants—their successful competitors—and towards the Protectorate administration which limited the profitability of the commercial crops. These frustrated elements had a minimal education (although some of them were college graduates). Most of them had plots of land in various districts, but had gravitated towards the "city," being the sons of chiefs (since 1926 a function no longer inherited), or adventurers, "entrepreneurs," landless persons, or simply marginal individuals. Many of them were not permanent town residents, but wandered all over the territory, and were potential agents of various ideas and organizations. But there were also in Katwe more "respectable" meeting places frequented by the African intelligentsia: physicians, lawyers, other university graduates (some of whom had studied abroad), writers, journalists, etc. There were also clubs established by local college graduates for sports and social events, as well as for the purpose of giving status and prestige to their members; the clubs also became foci of political organization. These were educational elites par excellence, and the leaders on the periphery *treated* them as such; they provided potential centers of competition with the British exogenous center and with the traditional separatistic sub-centers as well.

In spite of the fact that the elites were familiar with the prevalent Western and Eastern ideologies, which formed part of their identity and their orientations in the elitistic groups, they (except for the religious ones) never served as a factor in *mobilizing and activating* the periphery or even the intermediate agents and local "bosses."

Through a struggle for land ownership in Buganda, the traditional elites, the *Bataka,* achieved no tangible results; but one of the outcomes of this struggle was the very crystallization of these elements and the growth of a countrywide communication system between them.[15] This crystallization reached its peak with the establishment of a *Bataka* party in 1946. This was more in the nature of a populistic party, which by means of festivals and rituals (during which traditional costumes were worn, old-time dances were performed, and songs about "the good old days" were sung) activated numerous members—on the clan and *Miruka* level—and at the same time demonstrated its antagonism to the bureaucratic political framework of the Kabaka's court and his chiefs, civil servants (which constituted a subcenter). This party demanded, among other things, that the *Lukiko*, the Ganda "parliament," be made into a representative body, i.e., that the chiefs be elected; the assumption was that the representatives of the *Bataka* would be more popular. Yet the *Bataka* itself was a conspicuously ascriptive organization. Another idea which was strongly stressed was that of Buganda nationalism, and this led to somewhat ambivalent orientations towards the court of the Kabaka, who was himself a symbol of Buganda's special status. The party did not shun violence and took an active part in the 1949 riots.

The formation of the Uganda African Farmers' union began in 1947. The union was meant to be a sort of farmers' trade union, which opposed the government's fiscal policies, especially concerning the export and processing of cotton. The union was also designed to serve as the cooperative center of marketing and processing.

The Bataka party gave the union its full support, and the central personalities of the party were among the founders and active members of the union. Thus, when the 1949 riots began—spurred partly by the frustration following the union's failures and providing the focus for all the oppositionistic demands in Buganda (including separatistic aspirations) —these two organizations were considered to be the originators of the riots. The slogan used, "Su," was coined by the Bataka leadership. The revolt was partly against the court of the Kabaka, which later became the symbol of the very demands which the leaders of the organizations put forward, while many of them appeared in the party whose activities were destined to be in opposition. The revolt was suppressed by the military. The two organizations were declared to be communistic and were made illegal; some of the leaders were exiled.

In the middle of the fifties, there was a considerable intensification of efforts to organize political activity on the Western model. Many parties tries to organize (the Uganda Labour Party, the Uganda National Movement, the Uganda People's Party, the Democratic Party, the Progressive Party, etc.), but only a few of them could mobilize enough support. This intensified activity was apparently due to changes in neighboring countries and on the international scene (liberation movements in colonial countries and the beginning of the British colonial empire's disintegration in Africa).

In the meantime, the problem of the identity of the Buganda government and of the Kabaka's court became more acute. Until then it had been identified, according to Apter, with a set of archaic and anachronistic interests only, but in this structure there were latent factors which could change it from a sub-center simultaneously acting with other sub-centers into an independent one for the whole territory. Apparently there was a considerable readiness in the peripheries to accept the Buganda center, with some changes, as the general one. And since this structure had a tradition of adaptability and of an instrumental attitude, it could potentially become "a center." The British government, too, saw it as its heir, but Gubanda itself was undergoing an identity crisis and could not solve the dilemma between separatism (which wore a cloak for a neo-traditionalism) and the fulfillment of its functions as the "center."[16]

This dilemma split the largest and oldest of Uganda's parties—the Uganda National Congress—established in 1952 by leaders of the Bataka party and of the Farmers' union, who were joined by new elements from Katwe, and by new elements from outside Buganda. The UNC was composed of a central committee which included highly educated elites and of a network of local branches which were gradually set up all over the country. The key men of this party were the branch chairmen, usually recruited from among the more or less successful merchants, sons of chiefs who received no posts, and other persons whose mobility was cut off or blocked. Most of them were economic entrepreneurs, who, after initial successes, raised their level of expectations but were blocked by that "roof" of success which the structure assigned to Africans. They therefore transferred their entrepreneurship to the political field, although —in Apter's opinion—they saw it as a comedown. They were educated persons, but they were full of admiration for the members of the central committee in Katwa and were usually prepared to accept their authority. Nevertheless, each local branch was independent to a large extent and adapted itself to local conditions. This flexibility gave the party a great advantage: it was the first party which accommodated a large variety of groups and interests, as does the Western-type mass party. Although the branches were local, their attractiveness lay in their relationships with the *center*. Attempts to establish competing parties of an identical local character, without connection with the center, failed because they did not include symbols developed by the center, as center. Apparently, a collective super-tribal identity is sought by the Ugandans. For instance, members of the "Congress" in Toro dropped out of the party and tried to establish a competing party, *"Irka-Iwa-Toro,"* but failed completely.

There were, however, other parties on the political scene:

The Democratic Party, established in 1956 mainly by Catholic elements. Vague rightist tendencies earned it a "religious" label which prevented it from developing into a mass party, even though it gained many adherents all over the territory (especially since they gained an artificial majority in the elections to the Legislative Council held in 1961, which were boycotted by the Baganda traditionalists).

But already before that, in elections to the Constituent Assembly held in 1958, some of the elected representatives from the Northern regions organized themselves into a party which openly opposed Bagandan influence and Buganda's efforts to dominate the Federation or leave it altogether. This was the Uganda People's Union which began to attract adherents from among the non-Bagandan members of the UNC and of the Democratic Party. This party emerged mainly in reaction to the attitude of the traditional Ugandan elements and had no concrete aims or new ideas of its own.[17]

In 1960 Obote's faction united with the Uganda People's Union and formed the Uganda People's Congress. At that time, the realization that independence was drawing near made it possible for a sort of compromise to be reached between the old traditional elements and the local political structure. This compromise gave birth to the Kabaka Yekka party, which advocated the preservation of Buganda's special character within the federal structure of Uganda.

In elections held shortly before independence, the Uganda People's Congress won 43 seats (out of a total of 91 in the National Assembly), the Democratic Party and the Kabaka Yekka 24 seats each. Thus, it was necessary to form a coalition government, which included Obote's Congress Party and the Kabaka Yekka and stressed the "protestant Alliance" between the two parties.

As a result of this coalition, the separatist tendencies of Buganda—which apparently were due to the fear of losing traditional identity, as well as of having to share its material resources (Buganda was the richest unit in the territory)—were somewhat weakened. Participation in the center, combined with the preservation of the special interests and of a separate identity, seemed to provide the solution for the status of this kingdom. The appointment of the Kabaka as the President of Uganda symbolized and even assured a *de facto* solution. These arrangements also ensured the existence of a democratic government by maintaining a political center composed of a number of groups which could "balance" each other.

However, developments followed a different direction. The Congress party began to draw supporters from the other two parties, which grew smaller. According to Engholm and Mazrui,[18] a swift process of transition to a single-party government began to be noticeable, accelerated by the charismatic personality of Dr. Obote and the support of the military elite. The process was completed in 1966, when Buganda's privileges were abolished, the constitution was changed, the Kabaka was forced to go into exile and the country became a unitary state, with Milton Obote at its head, as a president with extensive powers.

Within a relatively short period of four years, four essential changes occurred in Uganda. First, the colonial exogenous center disappeared. Second, with its disappearance, the three-caste structure—along the lines of the skin colors of white, Indian and black—characteristic of the social system, was undermined. Third, elites, which had already been prepared as an alternative, set up a new center, which was not identical with any of the previous centers. Fourth, the center, in the process of crystallization, underwent processes of transformation, eliminating some of its local participants.

Between 1966-1971 Obote carried out the country's "move to the left" which was formalized when, in 1969, the UPC approved the "Common Man's Charter" which created in Uganda a one-party socialist declared state.

On May 1, 1970, despite the fact that the Ugandan economy had gone into a slump, Obote announced that the government would take over about 60 percent of all the country's major financial, commercial and industrial enterprises. All this to ensure, according to Obote, that "the production of wealth and its distribution should be controlled and managed with the active engagement of the people. . . . It is a revolution that aims at giving a new creed, new certainty, new sense of belonging . . ."[19]

Obote's "move to the left" effected mainly the Ganda, but the initiative and the achievements of the coup came entirely from the army's ranks—as a reaction to the competitive 1,000-man private army ("Presidential Protection Units") that was formed by Obote. Only post factum, after the completion of the coup d'état, did the army search for allies, and found them in the Baganda, and also in the other traditional units which Obote wanted to dissolve (except for his own Lango tribe), inter alia by the election system that was planned to cross the ethnic units—and by an appeal to the population's religious emotions (another previously tabooed area).

The efforts to renew the alliance between Buganda and Uganda were symbolized by the sending back to the country of the deceased *Kabaka*, and by according him "an unprecedented 73-gun salute—21 for an ex-president, 42 for a former king and 10 more for good measure."[20] Hitherto, it seemed that the main changes in President Amin's Uganda occurred at the ceremonial and symbolic level—except for the dissolution or weakening of the institutions that were directly identified with the Obote regime: e.g., the Presidential units, Adoko's General Service (the internal security), UPC, the National Service and the "Young Farmers" (an equivalent organization of Ghanaian "Young Pioneers").

In fact, the Ugandan Army, whose soldiers were recruited mostly from the northern regions (e.g., Acholi, Lango), seemed to appear for the first time as a "modern" stratum which could put its professional interest before its primoridal attachments and obligations. What a triumph to Dr. Obote's ideology!

This is, in outline, the "story" of Ugandan nation building and the formation of a new entity of collective identity. A basic question: how strong is its appeal? One of the basic dimensions and best predictors of attachment to integration in a collectivity seems to be the feeling of trust toward it.[21] In this sense Prewitt's[23] findings are surprisingly unequivocal; he asks a sample of about 280 adult education students (in Uganda of 1966), inter alia, the following question: "Some people are almost always fair and honest. It is safe to trust them. Other people, it is better not to trust. We cannot be too careful in how we deal with them. In general, can one trust the following people?"

The distribution of the responses was as follows:

Table 1. Attitude of social trust (in percentage)

	Always	Usually	Seldom	Never
Parents	60	30	5	0*
Teachers	42	45	6	1
Policemen	32	37	20	5
Civil servants	19	45	24	5
Army	17	32	30	15
Europeans	8	40	39	7
Africans	8	38	43	5
Indians	1	8	40	45

Source: Prewitt (1967: 65).
*The total is not 100% because between 5-7 percent did not answer.

Before we give a partial analysis of these findings, we must note that (according to Prewitt): "It was not feasible to ask each respondent to evaluate tribal grouping in Uganda. However, it was possible to ask him how much he trusted the Asian population, the Europeans, and his fellow Africans." We must emphasize the tremendous bias of the present sample: the subjects belonged to the "detribalized," relatively-modern narrow stratum. What is salient, is the great distance from, or "trust gap," vis-a-vis the Africans, who seem to be perceived as foreign inhabitants, that is, not belonging to the respondent ethnic group. Only the hated Indians, who were the traditional object of negative emotional responses, are more mistrusted. Even the Europeans seem to be more trusted than the African fellows.[23] The parents cannot be automatically taken, for our purpose, as the representatives of the whole "primordial collective," but such an interpretation in the African context does not seem far from true. The high degree of trust manifested towards the teachers, is seemingly (contrary to Prewitt's interpretation) rooted in the fact that most of the respondents themselves are prepared (and committed by the situation) for this role. But we must mention that "this question was also given to nearly 500 primary and secondary students in Uganda, and the pattern of responses remains amazingly stable."[24] Furthermore, in their self-image description—answering to the question "who am I"—46% of the respondents mentioned belonging either to their tribe, to their nation or to both. Of these, two-fifths either mentioned only their nation (or less than one-fifth from the total sample) or mentioned both, with the nation being cited first. The remaining three-fifths mentioned only their tribe or both, with tribe cited first.

THE AGRARIAN POLICIES OF THE CENTERS

The scope of the colonial government's interest in rural reconstruction seems to be limited and specific, but its intensity was probably high, despite the fact that reconstruction was carried out mainly through the existing traditional political system. The colonial center's interest seems to be "technical" and ad hoc in nature and consisted in the introduction of few cash crops, produced by the traditional production unit—the family farm. The cumulative results were deep and far-reaching, as will be demonstrated below. The ambitions of the post-colonial governments and their commitments to large-scale rural reconstruction were greater, but the obstacles were greater as well; the obstacles were greater not only because of the increase of the level of aspirations or because of the basic dilemma accompanying the giving of priority to rural development (against the other sectors), but also because the periphery developed a pattern akin to "reaction formation" mechanism.

Through interaction with the colonial (and later, independent) center, the most crucial process in our case study context occurs, vis., the crystallization and institutionalization of self-sufficient small agricultural units. This was a process of interplay between the pure subsistence economy and the introduction of new crops in Africa.

The earlier manifestation of the breakdown of the entirely subsistence-based economy occurred at the end of the nineteenth century, when some African "entrepreneurs" began selling forest products, e.g., timber, latex, oil plam and slaves. Thus an extracting economy was formed, i.e., a process of accumulation of goods without producing them through a technical transformation of inputs to outputs. Some of these entrepreneurs became wealthy by these activities on an individual basis and did not feel that they were violating the ideal of kinship unit autarchy. But it seems that such activities were qualitatively and quantitatively marginal, if not deviant; and the vast majority of the people continued to gather their food, and the savannah cultivators continued to grow their crops as their ancestors had done.

It is quite clear that in all colonial territories the passing from a pure subsistence economy toward a money and profit-making system was the direct consequence of contact with Europeans, and "in comparison with Kenya, conflict between natives and Europeans [in Uganda] is non-existent; the economic development is mainly the outcome of the natives' individual entrepreneurship, benefiting from the guidance of Europeans."[25] This quoted statement is only partly true. Both the English and French colonial systems were interested in the introduction of stable cash economy infrastructures in the territories. At first the French attempted to obligate the Africans to allocate a lot of land for cash plantations. This duty was perceived by the inhabitants as a component of the colonial coercive "package-deal," e.g., forced labor, poll taxes and other not quite intelligible new obligations. The fact that they could see their first cocoa crops only after five years of effort, contributed to the misunderstanding of the Administration's demands. The belief that any person who would plant a fruit tree—against Nature's will—would die when the first fruit would appear motivated Africans to boil the cocoa beans before they were planted or to abandon young plantations.

In Uganda the first period of cotton and coffee introduction was relatively modest, and this innovation met with considerable opposition, so that the colonial center needed the chiefs' political power to overcome many obstacles. The chiefs derived considerable profit from this innovation, not through direct economic activity but by activating the middle-range political set-up, i.e., in their capacity as tax collectors. It was only later, in their capacity as landlords and/or land leasers *(mailo)*,[26] that the chiefs derived direct economic profits from the commercial crops. The political center used fiscal systems and school fees as indirect means to influence the farmers to adopt a monetarizing system. Thus political and economic measures with economic incentives, combined to create a large stratum of "entrepreneurs."

The new center attempted to work for the rural periphery's improvement and reconstruction (within the framework of its limitations), especially because the rural sector is the single source of *resources for nation building* and for *recruitment of political support*. The recruitment of resources and the recruitment of political support were sometimes opposing processes, from the point of view of the rural sector.

An example of this policy was the bombastic scheme of so-called "Group Farming," that was born as a result of the rivalry between the Uganda People's Congress and the Democratic Party during the 1952 parliamentary election campaign (when the country achieved its independence). Both the UPC and DP appealed to farmers, especially through the marketing cooperatives, by promising tractors to relieve the drudgery of farm labor.[27] The promised pattern took account of the individualistic tendencies of most Ugandan farmers by retaining individual plots, and, in fact, the change would not be drastic, but only an extension of the existing cooperatives by tractorization and a more elaborated credit scheme.[28] In the *First Five-Year Development Plan* (1962) the group farming scheme was a pilot project and was located as a low priority experiment, following IBRID (1962) suggestions and the debates of a Symposium on Mechanical Cultivation, held at Makerere College. In 1963 —before any feedback came from the pilot scheme and before evaluation was possible—the government decided to quadruple the budget allocation to the project and even in a 1967 official document, when the total failure of the plan was already clear, it was proposed that by the end of the Second Five-Year Development Plan term there would be a total of 120 Group Farms, that would involve over half a million people.

Vail[29] argues that there are two reasons for this development: (a) the party hoped to use group farm activities as a medium for establishing its cells, and (b) to create a compelling *symbol of national development,* "an image in which progress would be identified with the governing party and its leaders." Vail adds: "It is not surprising that the Obote cabinet did not regard the Plan as gospel, but rather as a useful tool, selectively interpreted as the need arose, in the process of nation building. Economic development and political stability are interdependent in a non-authoritarian and federated nation, especially over the long run. But in the short run it seems likely that the power consolidation motive dominated over criteria of economic rationality in the decisions of Uganda political leaders—and that group farm policy can best be understood as part of a strategy of political development."

Only in July 1969 was there published (in *Uganda Argus*) an oppositionist PM's criticism on the rural reconstruction policy. He congratulated the Minister on the admission of the mistakes over group farms and wrote that this project had been spending public funds for nothing. He proposed that the group farms now in existence should immediately be transferred to the cooperative farming system, and that it had been wrong to put millions of shillings into such an experiment.

But in spite of its latent political aims, its faulty execution and the a priori social and economic misconceptions involved, the Group Farming scheme represented an attempt for large scale solutions of some endemic problems of the Ugandan rural sector:

- It enacted partially structural *land consolidation* through planning and arranging the plots in such a way that enabled attainment of the benefits of large scale cultivation. Concomitantly a campaign was conducted in favor of consolidation, but without great success, because it "failed to take account of the farmers' own views about land and the best ways of using it."[30] In addition to this there was the opening up of new land reserves and their allocation to the landless people, clearing them from the *tse-tse*, and irrigating them.[31] These were settlement projects, and, in fact, represented the institutionalization, or juridical recognition, of the customary habits of clearing the bush.
- The termination of the anomic situation of the customary land titles, by registration of these lands through the "Societies" (of marketing), i.e., the juridical body of the Group Farms.
- The improvement of the production techniques and marketing channels by supplying not only mechanical tools, but also technical assistance and consultation (by the so-called "Agricultural Extension Saturation Project"). But the density of the staffing—as was mentioned in the first section—was insufficient.

There were rarely any requests by the farmers to visit their farms, and it seems that their role is perceived more as being diffuse representatives or agents of the center rather than as sources for specific consultation. When the peasants were asked what help should be given by the government (which the local staff represents), 42.7% mentioned giving higher prices and another 27.7% preferred loans.[32] The Group Farms benefited more from the technical aid, but the basic attitude of the farmers toward the functions of the local experts did not seem to change.

From the inception of the Group Farming campaign, it was based—as we mentioned above—almost exclusively on cotton production. Obote's government is beginning to stress diversification of crops, but little is being done in this area. In the *Second Five-Year Development Plan* the four main crops for diversification were sugar, groundnuts, teak and tobacco, this as a counter balance to the price rise in the cotton and coffee world market prices.

The two five-year plans did not differ in any essential points of the development strategy, but some important points should be noted:

(1) The plans reflect the center's tendency towards greater centralization; while in the first plan the center participated to the extent of 59% of expenditure and economic activity, in the second plan the percentage rises to 70%.

(2) The budget rose by more than 100% (this is a great rise even taking into account the devaluation of the pound sterling), a fact which undoubtedly affected the rate of development. Although agriculture is the main source of this budget, it will only grow by 2-3% (its share in investment is 27%).

(3) The main trend of development—i.e., "balanced development"—is preserved, although emphasis is transferred to the development of the infrastructure and of the social services, the demand for which constantly becomes stronger.

(4) The goals of agriculture remain the same: productivization, diversification, development of credit plans to provide motivation for entrepreneurship but, as said before, the main emphasis is on the "cooperative farms."

(5) The forecasted increase in the amount of crops (to be achieved by a combination of soil improvement and enlargement of cultivated areas, use of pesticides, etc.), is fairly large: in cotton 32%, in coffee 27%; in the other secondary crops the increase is much larger. But in view of the expected drop in the prices of agricultural products on the world markets, the total increase from the sale of such products is estimated at 24%, which is only slightly more than the expected population increase.

However, behind the two "balanced" five year plans, we can discern the ever-growing dilemma with which the center is faced: Agriculture is the occupation of the great majority of the population. It provides the major part of the national production and income, yet it has not reached the stage at which it can support other sectors without impairing its own progress. Yet the center wants Uganda to become "a state based on a modern economy" (the Second Five-Year Plan), i.e., to industrialize it and to develop modern, social, educational and health services. The obstacles are well known, but the dilemma exists all the same.

INNER-DUALISM—A RESPONSE OF THE PERIPHERY

The main structural as well as psychological response of the African farmers in our case study to the pressure of reconstruction was the formation of a pattern of activity which may be called "inner dualism." By this we mean the simultaneous existence of two production systems, each based on soil as the main factor of production and one production unit, the kinship unit, but differing considerably in their economic aims, in their orientation towards the two systems, and in their social significance. Besides the traditional division between subsistence and cash crops, there was also a separate normative system and different expectations, and individuals acted simultaneously in both systems within the framework of a single socioeconomic unit.

This pattern was most clearly evident in those farms where the men raised coffee and cotton, marketed these crops and used the proceeds for the payment of taxes and school fees, and for the purchase of European-style clothing, bicycles, transistor radios and other "modern" consumption items. The women, on the other hand, raised maize, millet and the other foods meant for home consumption.

If any surplus of the food crops was accidentally produced, no effort was usually made to seel it, even if marketing facilities were available. One reason given was that men did not like women bringing money into the house, fearing that this would be perceived as a return of the bride price and might cause a weakening of masculine authority, which in turn would endanger the kinship group.[33] In Kisoga, for example, it is noted that the custom is to give permanent laborers plots of land (as gift) to grow subsistence crops, but not cash crops, and to build houses on.[34]

Several other manifestations, on the macro-economic level, of this phenomenon were a permanent and apparently institutionalized *wastage* of surplus food crops which already found their way to the marketing channels. This was one of the causes of the rapid rise of food crop prices caused by the formation of the growing urban sector's demands and the inability of the farmers to produce (or market) crops for the purpose of sale. So, the more an African country possessed a more developed cash crop industry, the more it became dependent on the import of foods from the neighbouring, less developed countries.

A complete dualism, i.e., a total differentiation between the two kinds of crops, should be viewed only as an "ideal type" (in the Weberian sense), seldom to be found, and even when found, warped in the process of continuing social changes and/or their differential crystallization in various places. But inner dualism seems to be a central phenomenon in our case analysis.

A certain degree of "dualism" can be found in a majority of agro-economic units of Uganda. It is thus possible to classify "dualism" into three levels or categories:

First, planning the allocation of plots on which subsistence crops will be grown so that sufficient food can be provided for the autarchic unit, while adding a large margin of surplus (if possible) to ensure against drought or other natural disasters. The size of the autarchic unit can vary, depending on the social structure of the observed system, and so does not necessarily imply the self-sufficiency of every family, as the ultimate consuming unit. The pattern does not exclude various forms of exchange (and even trade) within and between villages, and some degree of division of labor. The achieved surpluses are thus stored (insofar as possible) or destroyed, within the unit, either because no market or suitable marketing channels are at hand, or because the inhabitants lack a marketing orientation.

Second, emotional and/or value differentiation can be observed between the two systems: subsistence crops symbolize the continuity and the very existence of the effective kinship group, while cash crops are conditioned towards the "outside world" with its different interaction and value orientation patterns. There are two reasons for these beliefs. First, activities carried out in the monetary world are characterized by the laws of supply and demand, individual achievement criteria, and specificity and universality. Also, payment includes a series of items connected uniquely with the "modern world," items which sometimes are conspicuous representatives of this world, embodying its ambivalent nature, alien and attractive at the same time.

Third, when this differentiation is extended to the traditional sexual division of labor, it acquires universalistic and deterministic dimensions, with a permanence which is apparently unquestionable.

We would like to emphasize that the term "dualism" is not being used in the sense in which it is usually used in the literature.[35] We are not dealing here with two entirely separate and mutually exclusive socio-economic systems, connected only by a common political framework. The phenomenon becomes salient precisely because segregation is not carried out to a high degree and it is the *individual himself*, or the primary group, which becomes the focus of pressures, creating a situation which is psychologically somewhat similar to role conflict. Fallers, in his analysis of Ugandan chiefs' activities,[36] draws nearer to our interpretation; but the phenomenon seems to be much more widespread, extending to all strata and to other societal institutions.

Our argument is that the *inner dualistic* pattern makes use of traditional components, not of some of the components of change (as was done in the case of Japan, for instance) but of "protected bases" which reduce the levels of risk and anxiety aroused by alternative activities.

But in the attempt to understand the whole pehnomenon, we must take into consideration two other kinds of activities, on the same unit level, that function as alternatives to both subsistence and money-profit instrumental activities: (1) "Social" activities, e.g., participation in customary ceremonies and funerals, quasi-political acts, disputes, etc., and (2) leisure preferences,[37] common-beer-drinking and so on.

Both today and in earlier periods it is common practice to pin the problem of the underdeveloped countries on their value systems, as well as on "personality features" that give priority to "prestige-motives" against "material profit motive," or the inability to isolate the commitments to business success from other orientations that may distort its perspectives. Or, to quote Mazrui: "It is true that the African businessman sometimes attends an initiation ceremony or funeral during business hours rather reluctantly. And so what is at stake is not simply the businessman's unwillingness to evoke the excuse of "pressure of business" as a rationalization of his absence from a funeral. What is even more important as an inhibiting factor is the inability, or the presumed inability of the rest of his kin, to accept such an excuse as a legitimate one."[38]

In a given situation this priority of goals can be entirely rational. When the increase of money income is perceived to be opposed to the security of food supply, enhancement of one's prestige in the community, or maintenance of social harmony, or in the case in which one can depend on the aid of a large kinship group for seasonal farming activities (Including cash crop growing), the preference for "anti-economic" activities may be self-evident, according to the western criteria of "rationality" as well.

Returning to the earlier colonial period, we assume that the Africans have not learned and conditioned the *direct relationship* between (1) quantity of work inputs, (2) money requirements, and (3) constant values of this money purchasing power. Therefore money cannot be used as a secondary reinforcer or as an index of self-identity, i.e., as a test of how well one is doing one's job. There are some causes for these detachments.

The endemic instability and fluctuations of the cash crop prices (sometimes changing yearly in 100%), put the peasant, who was incapable of thinking in terms of the "world market" and of grasping other factors included in the "world-of-supply-and-demand," in a position of uncertainty. The nature of the modern monetary world is partly expressed in the fact that the individual acting in it can plan ahead and predict a considerable part of the results of his activities. There are many unknowns, to be sure, but they can usually be solved. The African accepted and was accepted into a *partly* monetary world, and therefore a distorted one. He did not have recourse to transcendental attitudes, but looked for more "intelligible" causes of price fluctuations, i.e., exploitation, and found them in the personality of the Asians and Europeans who paid for his crops. The immediate structural response was the inner dualistic pattern which ensured his basic survival. Since it was impossible to think of crops as a fixed factor (i.e., a predictable relationship between the amount of resources invested and the outputs of the investment), even in the subsistence sphere, it seems that the yields continued to be something strange and alien.[39]

This extremely limited consumption items, goods, and needs that it was possible to change for the currency. So the money's "translator" and "amplifier" qualities[40] and their level of generalization—i.e., the extent that any and all goods and/or services can be exchanged—was very low.[41] Connected but not directly derived from this was the relatively limited sense of "money-wealth" as such in the stratificational structure of these societies.[42] The strong connection between (1) inputs of work for cash crops, (2) taxation, or alternatively (3) diverse kinds of coercive work (e.g., *corvée*), and the perception of manual work for those outside the kin group as slavery (ILO, 1958: 148).

To be sure, the Africans long ago manifested a hypersensitivity to money profit making *as such*. The peasantry in the world at large usually identifies with the most traditional and conservative elements of their society, not only through its values and style of life, but also, as derived from these, in the kinds and species of cultivated crops. The African peasantry's "openness," on this level, is most impressive. An example of this is maize, an important staple in the local diet in Uganda, but not very "popular" with the experts of the local Ministry of Agriculture, since it was usually grown together with cotton, a process which impoverished the soil and increased erosion; between the years 1944-52 the amount of land under maize was fixed and peasants were allotted about 300,000 acres for it. But in 1953, when in neighbouring Kenya most of the maize crop was destroyed and the Protectorate administration undertook to buy any amount of maize at a fixed price, the area under maize increased by more than 100%. The government, however, was not prepared to buy such an amount, great surpluses were created, and the following year the area under maize not only went back to its previous size, but its rate of increase, as compared with other subsistence crops, even dropped.

Here, the strong intervention by the political center was not successful in inducing a tendency to move toward a new pattern of rural unit: family farming which renounces the "ideal" of autarchy by being based mainly on the mechanism of social labour division and specialization regulated by a developed market and monetary system but especially based on the belief in the functioning of such mechanisms. This is necessarily one pole of a supposed continuum, whose opposite pole is the unit based exclusively on food crop production as an economic and social fact, and whose intermediate stage is *inner dualism.* In our case such a development is not a necessarily a "natural" one. As will be seen below, the two types of activities—subsistence and cash—are not undertaken at the expense of one another, a situation which would arise if the two were at the opposite ends of a continuum.

Because the land resource allocation in each society was never *Pareto optimal* on the macro-economic level, the expansion of cash crops does not require a diminished allocation for subsistence crops (even though on a regional or familial-farm level such a dilemma can exist). On the contrary, the two systems tend to develop side by side. This was not only a consequence of land abundance, but mainly a result of connection between the two systems, as is manifested in Table 2.

Table 2. *The expansion of the main cash and subsistence crops*[a] *in Uganda, 1960-67*

Year	Cash crops[b]	Expansion index	Subsistence crops[b]	Expansion index	Cash/Food ratio
1960	2,162	100	5,975	100	.36
1961	2,660	122	6,690	112	.39
1962	2,426	112	6,732	113	.36
1963	2,658	123	6,376	107	.41
1964	2,766	128	7,152	120	.38
1966	2,948	135	7,194	120	.40
1967	2,980	135	–	–	–

Computed from Republic of Uganda, *1968 Statistical Abstract*, Ministry of Planning and Economic Development, Entebbe, 1968, p. 39.

(a) The cash crops include coffee (exclude estate coffee), cotton, tobacco; the subsistence crops were plantains, maize millet, groundnuts, beans, sweet potatoes, and cassava.
(b) In thousand acres.

The comparison of the two systems' growth can be summarized as follows:

(1) Over the years, there was a continuous growth in land exploitation (averaging 5% in cash crops and 6.6% on food crops) at a greater rate than the population increase (2.5% per annum).

(2) A great instability, or perhaps "flexibility," in land cultivation. Variations of (+)22% or (−)10% (see Table 3) are far from random or marginal oscillations. But the range of "negative" change is more limited in the subsistence sector

(−5%) than in the cash system (−10%). This can be interpreted as greater stability in the former, and it conforms with—or at least does not contradict—our perception of the subsistence system meaning.

Table 3. The yearly oscillations of land exploitation are presented in percentages.

Period	Cash crops area	Food crops area
1960-1	+22	+12
1961-2	−10	− 1
1962-3	+11	− 5
1963-4	+ 5	+13
1964-5	+ 7	0
1965-6	+ 3	+21
1966-7	− 3	

Source: Computed from Table 2.

(3) Against the background of this instability *within* both systems, the relatively low fluctuations in the ratio between cash and subsistence crop areas between the years are more salient. So one may assume a connection within the system as well as a differentiation ("dualism") between the two systems.

(4) In Uganda, when the land allocation is taken as index, the dominant activities remain the subsistence activities. Uganda (according to 1964 data) allocated .39 acres per capita of the population for cash crops and about 1 acre for subsistence crops.

THE EXTENSION OF THE INNER DUALISTIC PATTERN

Precisely because the dualism does not operate as indicated by its original definition, the pattern tends to spread to other societal spheres and institutions and have an effect on them. But what makes this phenomenon crucial, is the inner dualistic character of the major linking mechanism between the center and its peripheries as well. The center itself is successful in its exercise of power to the extent that it can perform its roles in both systems. In other words, the dualism seems to be inherent in the major political, economic, and expressive roles and institutions.

For example, H. S. Aynore describes in his *Notes from Africa*[43] the figure of a young African politician: extremely intelligent and sensitive, with a perfect Western education (the result of many years in Paris), culturally westernized, a man of the world, highly involved in his country's good. But when the writer occasionally met him in his clan milieu, he found before him a completely different man, guided by a completely different set of rules. The African was fully aware of his "duality" and apologetically explained to his white colleague, that his power and position in the capital (i.e., center) were, in fact, dependent on his position among his ethnic group and its support, but that irrespective of this fact, he himself was highly involved in this world and committed to its rules (e.g., he divorced his modern, well educated and beautiful African wife, and took a simple clan girl, according to his customary obligations; or, when his relatives arrived in the capital, he felt he had to act towards them in accordance with the customary diffuse obligations).

Thus, the dependence of the center on its peripheries was not only instrumental (e.g., taxes taken, manpower mobilization, political support, etc.) but also psychological. In this case it is not self-evident that the center "is the center of the order of symbols, of values and beliefs which govern the society."[44] The peripheries are not only self-sufficient in this domain, but seemingly are used by the diverse components of the center as a reference culture, in various situations.

In spite of this, the center must act towards the reconstruction and improvement of the peripheries' economic and social conditions, the more so if it is committed to a strong ideology of development and modernization. But, most acts of the center must be compatible with the periphery's will or tradition and must avoid too intensive an effort at mobilization, which--contrary to what is commonly thought-"enhances destructive social and political division and threatens the common national basis,"[45] and other entities,[46] even if this is in its power.

What the real power of this center and the scope of its activities are, is not easy to estimate, and this strength changes from time to time and from issue to issue. In 1966 Prewitt[47] asked students which of the following statements was most true (we give the distribution of the response frequencies in brackets): (1) People who break laws seldom get away (18%), (2) People who break laws only sometimes get away (44%), (3) People who break laws usually get away (32%). It is presumed that this question refers not only to the efficiency of the police: only 18% assumed that all offenses against the center (law) were punished, as opposed to 32% who believed the center can or will not react against the offenders. Moreover, we can learn something about the legitimacy of the center from the data obtained by Prewitt (see Table 4).

The unusual concentration of the answers around the extremes,

Table 4. The right to oppose a law (if it is perceived as immoral)

Question	N	Very true	Somewhat true	Not very true	Not at all true
If someone is convinced a law is immoral, does he have the right to disobey it?	280	31%	17%	14%	35%

Source: Prewitt (1967: 61).

seem to hint at the strong emotional aspect of the problem.[48] Prewitt attributes this to the religious (Christian) feelings of the respondents, while we tend more to attribute it to an additional set of norms and rules that exists side by side with the "modern civic sentiments"—that is, the customary norms which serve as a model for "morality."

What is the role of the educational system in preserving or disrupting this pattern of inner dualism? Education is the sui generis melting point between the center and peripheries; education is perceived as an immense mechanism which creates the "nation-wide sentiments."[49] From the viewpoint of the individual and his family, schooling has been almost the only route to personal advancement and mobility, and is seen as a worthwhile investment (e.g., a girl who is educated commands a proportionate bride-wealth).[50] But there is no evidence that education—in terms of its curriculum content—is working against the dualism. Evans, in a sample of 32 secondary schools, found very modest achievements in the process of internalization of national goals, in spite of what seems to be success in structural mixing of pupils of different tribal and ethnic backgrounds as a policy of the center: a full 35% of the sample schools never sing the national anthem; only 19% observed any form of ceremonies to mark Independence Day, but 80% of the schools frequently or occasionally allocated time to debate topics of national interest.[51] Moris is unequivocal: "It was our impression that the East African government have succeeded in 'getting across' the concern for nation-building much more than they are aware. Students mentioned the aspect of nation-building quite frequently in answer to various questions, and a smaller number seemed sincere in their consideration of this aspect in choosing careers. On the whole, however, the concern about nation-building (no matter how sincerely given) seemed vague and unrelated to students' personal lives. Schools have not mobilized their students in this connection: they have been unable to make the issue a real one."[52]

One index of relation toward both the ingredients of the duality, is the extent and place of use of the native languages. Evans shows that nearly half the schools require English to be spoken at all times (and not only in the classroom), and about 30% also punished those using the vernacular.[53]

Precisely this expulsion of the vernacular from the schools, reinforces the duality through the cognitive differentiation of the "new-knowledge" from the initial identities of the pupils. Another surprising consequence of this policy is the great horizontal mobility among the occupations, and what seems to be the lack of perception of a profession as a "calling," because the field that one has specialized in (e.g., agriculture) is less important than the fact that one holds any of the "new-knowledges."

Uganda, like other quasi-modern political systems, has its administrative apparatus, which embraces the whole country. This network is composed of two-fold strata: (1) the local–district level–government, a residue of the British policy of *indirect rule*, i.e., government by means of indigenous institutions, (2) the representatives of the central government's diverse ministries. Both have crucial roles, as Sathyamurthy assumes "the district level of administration represents the most crucial link between national goals and the microcosmic, tribally differentiated, religiously fragmented and politically competitive rural society. The district level of administration in Uganda serves as *the* channel of communications through which commands flow to the periphery, central policy is explained to local politicians and the local people at large, and such central policies as directly affect the regions are executed."[54]

But these two bodies serve not only as channels of symbolic and political communication flow, but also as foci for mobilization of resources from—and reallocation to—the peripheries, as well as foci of diverse demands and power aggregation twoard the center. What seems to be very significant in this context is the different roles of the same institutions in the "poor" northern districts (e.g., Acholi, Lango, Bunyoro) and those of the southern "rich" areas (i.e., Buganda, and Busogo). Weintraub differentiated between a center which possesses autonomous resources and a center which must base itself on mobilization systems. Here we see a center that appears before several peripheries as possessor or controller of resources and before others mainly as "absorber."[55] (Of course, such a duality is involved in all modern government, and especially in those of welfare-state systems, when it takes from the well-to-do and gives to the weak, but here the presented pattern is different, taking account of the segments that were cut by these relations.)

In the former case, the local authority could levy taxes on the people and could pass laws, but it could not raise sufficient money to run the district services. In this case, the center had to intervene with grants-in-aid or by sending officers to the district administration. To this extent, the central government was the one developing the district.⁵⁶ The fact that the district administrations were not self-sufficient contributed to the process of making them a branch of the central government or of the ruled Congress Party,⁵⁷ in spite of the fact that the district administration is responsible for many of the most important services affecting the ordinary man.⁵⁸

An important item in the growth of expenditures of district administrations has been the overhead costs of politicizing the eminent local "personalities," i.e., the salaries and allowances to the notables, since there is no tradition of voluntary or amateur participation in leadership roles concerned with any outside or *modern* items (i.e., non-customary). The leaders that received their position by tradition were usually ready to enter in exchange situations with the "new system," through manipulation of their "old" resources, but demanded the rewards in "new currency." This is another version of what we called *inner dualism,* when it is transferred to an additional sphere (i.e., politics). The African pattern of urbanization—the moving to the cities for purposes of money (or other "modern items") earning, and returning to the clan—can be seen as an extension of the cash crop component of dualism.⁵⁹

Teachers' roles were usually taken as located in the vital position of expressive leadership and as *locum tenens* of the center in the periphery. But the role of the school system, as propagator of the center's messages and symbols, is doubtful,⁶⁰ perhaps because the educational system was seemingly more attached to its religious background, according to the traditional affiliation of the schools to missionary services. But this seems to be an additional consequence of the duality's "latent structure" (in the Lazarsfeld sense), i.e., the center (sometimes through its local extensions and agents) maintains a large scale, give-and-take relationship with the peripheries, but this tends to be restricted—much more than in the western systems—to the instrumental and financial spheres. *In this case, the center itself is perceived as belonging only to one component of the inner dualism external to the definition of identity and the sense of belonging of the majority of individuals who compose the periphery, as well as to the more operative social units (the farm, clan, and tribe).*

CONCLUSIONS

The confrontation between the two perceptions according to the intensity and the scope of the center's involvement in the process of rural reconstruction in Uganda seems to be fruitful. The perception of the center as a potentially omnipotent and all-embracing entity as opposed to the conception that can be represented by the Antoine de Saint-Exupéry sage Emperor, who commanded the sun to set and rise exactly when the time came—and thus maintained his absolute authority over the whole universe—poses the problem acutely. Without making any far-reaching generalizations, it can be argued that the latter model is more appropriate to the Ugandan reality, not because the periphery is not responsive (as is frequently argued in the literature) but precisely because of its responsiveness.

The reaction pattern of the periphery raises some questions. To what extent can the emergence of this pattern of segregation be seen as a "pathological" phenomenon, liable to freeze all changes by becoming exogamous to the system; or as a transformative mechanism which, by using traditional aspects, achieves large measures of flexibility in absorbing change while shielding the general system from severe upheavals.

These reaction patterns may be interpreted both as a partial, gradual and flexibile response to external pressure and as a mechanism of self-defense demonstrating unequivocal desire to maintain the basic features of the traditional village. Both interpretations may be correct. In any event they are not mutually exclusive. The adequacy of each of the interpretations varies from society to society, from area to area within the same society and from period to period within the same population. The optimistic interpretation, i.e., that which percieves the inner dualism as a reflection of consent of willingness to accept, at least partly, the demands of the center emphasizes the positive potential in inner dualism. It is suggested in this case to regard inner dualism as a transitional stage which enables a gradual transformation, thus avoiding the by-products of social and political deterioration which is so common in many developing countries. The second interpretation—the pessimistic one—probably indicates that inner dualism at least in its stage of institutionalization is a manifestation of stagnation and the periphery's inability to reach the take-off level.

The adequate interpretation of inner dualism has implications beyond the interest of academic scholars. After all, misinterpretations on the part of scholars do not produce any critical results. However, the diagnostic skill of the political leadershp may have far-reaching results on the character and the scope of rural reconstruction. In other words, a political elite which adopts the optimistic interpretation would probably pursue a policy different in many aspects from that pursued by an elite which adopts a negative attitude towards inner dualism. As a matter of fact the essence of the interpretation is an indivisible part of the political and ideological characteristics of the center in general and of its conception of center-periphery relations in particular.

Our specific interest was in the analysis of inner dualism in the

Ugandan society as a reflection of a particular pattern of interaction between the different historical power-centers that were present in different periods in Uganda and the rural periphery. Needless to say, the history of relationships were not always harmonious. The obstacles on the way to harmonious coexistence were enormous: among them, scarcity of economic resources and other means of production, organizational ineptitude, and religious-ethnic-tribal conflicts. No less significant are the symbolic-cultural obstacles. Many of the stumbling-blocks in the way of modernization of the rural sector refer to the cultural traditions of the rural society. True, tradition in general determines the nature and the range of the creativity and innovation of the society. However, the extent of traditionalism and its impact on the range of innovation is not uniform. There is an abundance of evidence about the existence of different types of traditions. In any case, it seems that inner-dualism is a clear evidence both to the innovation potential of tradition and to its conservative power.

NOTES

1. Edward Shils "Center and Periphery" (London: Routledge and Kegan Paul, 1961), p. 117.
2. In addition, the semantic analysis of the term "periphery," leads to associations of unimportance, powerlessness, or marginality.
3. See for example: Almond and Coleman (1960), Levy (1966: 290-374), Apter (1965), Ake (1967), and Shils (1958).
4. Shils, op. cit., p. 125.
5. Usually, this identity is based on so-called primoridal ties (Shils, 1958, or Geertz, 1963), but it is insufficient to define it thus because the identity supplied by the center is not necessarily antithethical "civil"). In many cases, the collective identity proposed by the center also has strong primordial ingredients.
6. Some Latin American centers have declared their intentions for comprehensive rural reconstruction, but their readiness—or ability—to resort to force in order to achieve their plans is non-existent or exists only to a very limited extent, except for the cases of Cuba and Mexico.
7. It seems that among modern societies the unique example in which the rural sector—at least ideologically—tended to remold the whole system, is the Jewish settlement in pre-independence Israel. See Weintraub, Lissak and Azmon (1969).
8. For many years the income per capita in Uganda oscillated around 25 pound Sterling per annum, the Gross National Product per head is £27, and the increases in food products and goods hardly matched the increased number of consumers (the growth rate of the population is 2.5% per year). In 1968, from about 8 million people, only 281,800 (or 3.5%) were on the employment payroll in both private and public sectors. The dominant characteristic of the Ugandan economical as well as social structure is not only its total dependence on the primary sector productions

(subsistence and cash), but the fact that in spite of the proclaimed official policy of creating a "balanced" economy, this is a peasant society not only by its structure but, as we shall see, by its basic orientations. The cotton and coffee introduced Uganda into the modern world economy about a hundred years ago, but in spite of the rapid growth of the export of these crops, Uganda is not considered a significant factor in the world market, as are Ghana (which in 1967-68 produced 32% of the total cocoa production of the world, and thus holds the first place) or the Ivory Coast (the third coffee producer in the world, after Brazil and Colombia).

9. S. N. Eisenstadt, "Institutional and social aspects of agricultural development and modernization," in Shapiro (ed.) Rural Settlements of New Immigrants in Israel (Rehovot: Settlement Study Center, Keter Publishing House, 1971), p. 8.

10. For a systematic analytical description of the possible varieties of interaction between a societal center and rural periphery, see Weintraub (1970).

11. For a very detailed description and excellent analysis of this process, see Apter (1967), Fallers (1950), and Low and Pratt (1950).

12. David E. Apter, *The Political Kingdom in Uganda* (New Jersey: Princeton University Press, 1967).

13. F. B. Welbourn, *Religion and Politics in Uganda 1952-1962*, East African Publishing House, 1965.

14. Apter, op. cit., pp. 244-247.

15. For the analysis of the land tenure system and its impact on the social process which occurred in Uganda, see the forthcoming study of comparative analysis of agricultural development and modernization.

16. J. M. Lee, "Buganda's position in federal Uganda," Journal of Commonwealth Political Studies, Vol. III, No. 3 (1965).

17. D. A. Low, *Political Parties in Uganda, 1949-1962* (London: Athlon Press, 1962).

18. G. F. Engholm and Ali Mazrui, "Violent constitutionalism in Uganda," Government and Opposition, Vol. II, No. 4, pp. 585-598.

19. Milton A. Obote in *Uganda Argus,* May 2, 1970.

20. Time, April 13, 1971.

21. Michael Inbar and Baruch Kimmerling, *Social Integration and Trust* (forthcoming).

22. Kenneth Prewitt, "Political perspectives of opinion leaders in Uganda," Social Science Information, Vol. XLVI, No. 2, pp. 53-78.

23. H. S. Morris, *The Indians in Uganda* (London: Weidenfeld and Nicolson, 1968).

24. Prewitt, op. cit.

25. S. H. Frankel, *Capital Investment in Africa* (London: Oxford University Press, 1938), p. 259.

26. H. M. West, *The Mailo System in Buganda* (Entebbe: The Government Printer, 1964).

27. David Vail, "Group farming and statecraft in Uganda," Makerere University College: Rural Development Research Papers No. 71, Economic Research Seminar (Mimeographed), 1968, pp. 8-9.

28. Charsley, 1966, p. 1.

29. Vail, op. cit., p. 10.

30. Beverly Brock, "Customary land tenure, 'industrialization' and agricultural development: some comments on a conference," Kampala: RDR Papers (mimeographed), 1968, p. 15.

31. See Yeld (1965), Apthorpe (1966), Hall (1968), and Jiwani (1968).

32. E. R. Watts, "Staffing aspects of the extension saturation projects in Uganda," Makerere University College: Rural Development Research Papers No. 90 (mimeographed), p. 9.

33. Ann Martin, "The marketing of minor crops in Uganda," London: HMSO (mimeographed), 1963, p. 3.

34. Harmsworth, 1962, p. 6.

35. See, for example, Bock (1961), Nash (1964), McLaughlin (1966).

36. Lloyd A. Fallers, "The predicament of the modern African chief: an instance from Uganda," American Anthropologist, Vol. LVII (1955), pp. 290-305.

37. The frequent argument that the appearance of unemployment in developing countries is only a process whereby latent rural unemployment becomes evident is incorrect because the so-called "rural unemployment" is frequently leisure, and this is the exact opposite. In an area where favourable natural resources and social milieu offer opportunity, leisure can be perceived as a "higher standard of living" (Brock, op. cit., p. 13).

38. Ali A. Mazrui, "Political culture and economic socialization in East Africa," Dar-es-Salem: EA Social Council (mimeographed), 1968, p. 7.

39. But, on the other hand, the subject of cash crop prices became the nucleus of the creation of an African collective identity, which perhaps later had a "positive" function in promoting solidarity beyond the local ethnic, tribal and political units, and even cut across the African social strata. For example, the price of cotton was a common problem and became a common interest for the Baganda, the Itso (Taso tribesmen), the *bakopi* (peasants, tenants) and the *bantogola* (landlord) in Uganda.

40. Marshal McLuhan, *Understanding Media: The Extension of Man* (New York: McGraw-Hill, 1965).

41. Marion J. Levy, *Modernization and the Structure of Societies* (New Jersey: Princeton University Press, 1966), pp. 257-262.

42. Fallers (1964) has stressed the point that man has a tendency to see himself in dyadic relationships; i.e., to compare himself to another individual who is either his chief or his client, representing a lack of overall concepts of classes or strata in which to place an individual human being.

43. Tel-Aviv: Am Oved (Hebrew), 1971.

44. Shils, op. cit., p. 117.

45. Moshe Lissak, "Some theoretical implications of the multidimensional concept of modernization," International Journal of Comparative Sociology, Vol. XI, No. 3 (1970), p. 205.

46. In this sense, one can understand Amin's almost unique principled argumentation, when he tried to justify his coup. He attached principles of the National Service—the main mechanism that Obote tried to build for the purpose of intensive and large-scale mobilization: "When it came to proposals for National Service, it was obvious that Obote did not have the interest of the Common Man at heart. Obote proposed that 'all able bodied persions' should spend at least two years in a National Service camp, far away from their home districts . . . The people were not paid for their work . . . [and it is] wondered how a self employed individual would for that period meet his expenses . . . Obote totally ignored the social problems that would inevitably arise if his proposals were put into effect, especially those relating to the split family." (*Uganda Argus*, 28.1.71).

47. Prewitt, op. cit., p. 61.

48. Another interesting split of the sample occurred when the subjects were asked the question "which man helps his country more: (a) the man who does not

pay his taxes so he can use the money for his children's school fees (44%), (b) the man who pays his taxes but then cannot pay for his children's school fees" (51%); 5% no information or responses. Ibid.

49. Musgrove (1962), Castle (1963), and Nekyon (1967).

50. Fred K. Kamoga, "School leaving as affected by separation of parents," Kampola: Conference Papers no. 203, 1963, p. 4. There are some bottlenecks in this system: (a) only about half the 6-14 age-group benefits (1967 data) from some elementary education, with boys in the majority; 642,000 children were enrolled in primary schools; (b) of the children in the senior secondary age group (estimated by us as about 581,000 in number), only 6% were registered in various senior secondary schools (including teacher training, technical and commercial colleges). This in spite of the recent policy to pass the majority of the pupils sitting for the primary examinations, but to divide leaving levels to two. Thus, out of over 73,000 pupils who sat for the 1969 examination, 66,500 passed, but of these only 9,186 obtained a first grade pass, which secures their chances to enter secondary classes (*Uganda Argus*, January 7, 1970); (c) the tendencies that were observed in 1958 by Goldthrope and MacPherson —i.e., the reduction of the proportion of Baganda in the total enrollment and the spread of the graduates over the whole occupational spectrum (in contrast to the gravitation towards the law in the other underdeveloped areas)—seem to continue, but the whole higher educational system is still very small. In 1967-68 1,467 students were registered at Makerere University, an increase of about 55% compared with 1960-61, a great relative increase but one that is far from adequate in fulfilling the needs. But already in 1964 there were 2,257 students abroad. The majority studied education, nursing and medicine, but there were also students of engineering.

As elsewhere among the new nations, the building of a formal educational system has been given relative primacy by the political center and education has been regarded as crucial. During 1968-69 25% of the central government expenditure was allocated to education (Republic of *Uganda,* 1969: 58) *pari passu* with a great effort to detach educational achievement from its status context or its ethnic conditioning, e.g., by "controlling" the number of pupils passing the examinations. In 1969, the higher failure rate, as in previous years, came from Buganda (16% against about 7% on the average for other regions) and Goldthrope and MacPherson (1958) described their candidates as "not only fewer in number but also relatively . . . less mature and experienced."

51. David R. Evans, "Secondary schools as agents of socialization for national goals," Makerere: Institute of Social Research, Conference Papers no. 466 (mimeographed), 1968.

52. Jon R. Moris, "The impact of secondary education upon student attitudes towards agriculture," Makerere: U.E.A. Social Science Conference, Conference Papers no. 372 (mimeographed), 1966, p. 16.

53. Evans, op. cit.

54. T. V. Sathyamurthy, "Center-local relationship at the district headquarters," Kampala: EAISR, Conference Papers, No. 380 (mimeographed), 1966, p. 1.

55. Weintraub, 1970, p. 371.

56. Isaac Ojok, "The relationship between central and local governments in Lango and Bunyoro," Makerere: EASRI, Conference Papers no. 367 (mimeographed), 1966, p. 3.

57. Another process that seemed to contribute to the decline of the local government's effective power and symbolic salience, was of course the achievement of independence, and through this the moving of the best cadres tword the center,

and thus "the present incumbents of various district departmental leaderships, including the district commissioner were generally less experienced, less qualified and educated, and perhaps less self-confident than their colonial predecessors" (Sathyamurthy, 1966).

58. Colin Leys, *Politicians and Policies: An Essay on Politics in Acholi, Uganda 1962-1965* (Nairobi: East African Publishing House, 1967), p. 23.

59. Baruch Kimmerling, "Subsistence crops, cash crops, and urbanization." Rural Sociology, Vol. XXXVI, No. 4 (1971).

60. Evans, op. cit.

REFERENCES

AKE, C. (1967) A Theory of Political Integration. Homewood: The Dorsey Press.
ALMOND, G. and J. COLEMAN (eds.) (1960) The Politics of Developing Areas. New Jersey: Princeton University Press.
APTER, D. E. (1967) The Political Kingdom in Uganda. New Jersey: Princeton University Press.
––– (1965) The Politics of Modernization. Chicago and London: The University of Chicago Press.
APTHORPE, R. (1968) Land Law and Land Policy in Eastern Africa. Paper for the conference on land law reform (available as "Sociology 72"), Kampala (mimeographed).
–––(1966) Survey of Land Settlement Schemes and Rural Development in East Africa. EAISR Conference paper. Kampala: East African Social Science Research Council, Makerere College (mimeographed).
AYNORE, H. S. (1971) Notes from Africa. Tel-Aviv: Am Oved (Hebrew).
BROCK, B. (1968) "Customary Land Tenure, 'Individualization' and Agricultural Development: Some Comments on a Conference." RDR Papers. Kampala (mimeographed).
CASTLE, E. B. (1963) Education in Uganda: The Report of the Uganda Education Commission. Entebbe: The Government Printer.
CHARSLEY, S. R. (1966) Group Farming in Bunyoro. Conference Papers, no. 248. Makerere: Institute of Social Research (mimeographed).
––– (1966) The Profitability of a Group Farm. Conference Papers, no. 405. Makerere: Institute of Social Research.
DEUTSCH, K. W. (1961) "Social Mobilization and Political Development." American Political Science Review, Vol. LV (September).
EISENSTADT, S. N. (1971) "Institutional and Social Aspects of Agricultural Development and Modernization," in O. Shapiro (ed.), Rural Settlements of New Immigrants in Israel. Rehovot: Settlement Study Center, Keter Publishing House.
––– (1966) Modernization: Protest and Change. Englewood-Cliffs: Prentice-Hall.
ELKAN, W. (1961) The Economic Development of Uganda. London: Oxford University Press.
ENGHOLM, G. F. and ALI MAZRUI (1967) "Violent Constitutionalism in Uganda." Government and Opposition, Vol. II, no. 4, pp. 585-598.
EVANS, D. R. (1968) "Secondary Schools as Agents of Socialization for National

Goals." Conference Papers (no. 466). Makerere: Institute of Social Research (mimeographed).

FALLERS, L. A. (1964) The King's Men. Leadership and Status in Buganda on the Eve of Independence. London, New York and Nairobi: EAISR and Oxford University Press.

——— (1955) "The Predicament of the Modern African Chief: An Instance from Uganda." American Anthropologist, Vol. LVII, pp. 290-305.

——— (1950) Bantu Bureaucracy. Cambridge: Haffner & Sons.

FALLERS, M. (1960) The Eastern Lacustrine Bantu. London: International African Institute.

FRANKEL, S. H. (1938) Capital Investment in Africa. London: Oxford University Press.

GAYER, C. M. A. (1957) "Report on Land Tenure in Bugisu," Land Tenure in Uganda. Entebbe: Government Printer.

GEERTZ, C. (1963) "The Integrative Revolution," in Geertz (ed.), Old Societies and New States. Glencoe: Free Press, pp. 105-157.

GIL, M. (n.d.) Agriculture in Uganda. Jerusalem: Ministry of Education and the Department of International Cooperation in the Ministry for Foreign Affairs (mimeographed).

GOFFMAN, E. (1959) The Presentation of Self in Everyday Life. New York: Doubleday.

GOLDTHORPE, J. E. and M. MacPherson (1958) "Makerere College and Its Old Students," Zaire, Vol. XII, no. 4.

HALL, M. (1968) "Agricultural Planning in Buganda 1963-1966." East African Journal of Rural Development. Vol. I, no. 1, pp. 52-69.

HARMSWORTH, J. (1962) The Economic Development of Uganda. Baltimore: Johns Hopkins University Press.

Her Majesty's Stationary Office (HMSO) (1955) East African Royal Commission 1953-1955 Report. London.

International Bank for Reconstruction and Development (IBRD) (1962) The Economic Development of Uganda. Baltimore: John Hopkins University Press.

International Labor Organization (1958)

INBAR, M. and B. KIMMERLING (forthcoming) Social Integration and Trust.

JIWANI, S. H. (1968) Agricultural Development Planning and Physical Environmental Data in Uganda. Rural Development Research Paper. Makerere: University College (mimeographed).

KAHL, J. A. (1968) The Measurement of Modernism. Austin. The University of Texas Press.

KAMOGA, F. K. (1963) School Leaving as Affected by Separation of Parents. Conference Papers (no. 203). Kampala.

KILLICK, T. (1966) "Sectors of Economy," in W. Birmingham, I. Neustadt and E. N. Omaboe (eds.). A Study of Contemporary Ghana. Vol. I. London: George Allen & Unwin.

KIMMERLING, B. (1971) "Subsistence Crops, Cash Crops and Urbanization." Rural Sociology, Vol. XXXVI, no. 4.

KIWENUKA, M. S. (1968) Nationality and Nationalism: The Buganda Case. USSC Conference Papers (no. 495, mimeographed).

LEE, J. M. (1965) "Buganda's Position in Federal Uganda." Journal of Commonwealth Political Studies. Vol. III, no. 3.

LEYS, C. (1967) Politicians and Policies. An Essay on Politics in Acholi, Uganda 1962-65. Nairobi: East African Publishing House.
LEVY, M. J. (Jr.) (1966) Modernization and the Structure of Societies. New Jersey: Princeton University Press.
LISSAK, M. (1970) "Some Theoretical Implications of the Multidimensional Concept of Modernization." International Journal of Comparative Sociology, Vol. XI, no. 3, pp. 195-207.
LOW, D. A. and R. C. PRATT (1960) Buganda and the British Overrule. London: Oxford University Press and EAISR.
LOW, D. A. (1962) Political Parties in Uganda, 1949-62. London University. London: Athlon Press.
LUYIMBAZI-ZAKA, S. J. (1962) "Educational Revolution in Uganda." The Challenge of Uganda's Second Five-Year Development Plan. Kampala: Obote Foundation.
MARTIN, A. (1963) The Marketing of Minor Crops in Uganda. London: HMSO (mimeographed).
MASEFIELD, G. B. (1962) Agricultural Change in Uganda, 1945-60. Food Research Institute. Stanford: Stanford University Press.
MAZRUI, Ali A. (1968) Political Culture and Economic Socialization in East Africa. Conference Papers. Dar-es-Salem: EA Social Council (mimeographed).
McLOUGHLIN, P. F. M. (1970) Notes on the Theory of Change Technology and the Concept of "Subsistence." Rural Development Research Seminar Paper.
− − − (1966) "Technological Change, 'Dual Economy'. Theory and the Problem of Development." Zeitschrift für Nationalökonomie. Vol. XXVI, no. 4.
McLUHAN, M. (1965) Understanding Media: The Extension of Man. New York: McGraw-Hill.
MEAD, D. C. (1967) "The Basis of Uganda's Economy." The Challenge of Uganda's Second Five-Year Development Plan. Kampala: Obote Foundation.
METTRICH, H. (1967) Aid in Uganda−Agriculture. London: Overseas Development Institute.
MIDDLETON, J. (1966) The Lugbara of Uganda. New York: Holt, Reinhart and Winston.
MORIS, J. R. (1966) The Impact of Secondary Education Upon Student Attitudes Towards Agriculture. Conference Papers (no. 372). Makerere: U.E.A. Social Science Conference (mimeographed).
− − − (1966) The Evaluation of Settlement Scheme Performance: A Sociological Appraisal. Social Science Conference Papers. Makerere: College University (mimeographed).
MORRIS, H. S. (1968) The Indians in Uganda. London. Weidenfeld and Nicolson.
MUKWAYA, A. B. (1957) The Rise of the Uganda African Farmers Union in Buganda, 1947-1949. Conference Papers, no. 75. Moshi: East African Institute of Social Research (mimeographed).
MUSGROVE, F. (1952) "A Uganda Secondary School as a Field of Cultural Change." Africa. Vol. XXII no. 3, pp. 234-249.
NASH, N. (1964) "Southeast Asian Society: Dual or Multiple." JAS. May, pp. 417-23.
NEKYON, A. A. (1967) "The Agricultural Revolution in the Second Five-Year Development Plan." The Challenge of Uganda's Second Five-Year Development Plan. Kampala: Obote Foundation, pp. 70-77.
OBOTE, M. A. (1968)(?) The Common Man's Charter. Kampala: UPC Annual Delegates' Conference.

OJOK, I. (1966) The Relationship Between Central and Local Governments in Lango and Bunyoro. Conference Papers (no. 367). Makerere: EASRI (mimeographed).

OKEREKE, O. (1968) A Historical Outline of the Development of the Cooperative Movement in Uganda. Rural Development Papers (no. 59). Makerere: University College (mimeographed).

PTHIENO, T. M. and D. C. R. BELSHAW (1965) Technical Innovation in Two Systems of African Peasant Agriculture in Bukeei District, Uganda. Conference Papers (no. 335). Makerere University College (mimeographed).

PREWITT, K. (1967) "Political Perspectives of Opinion Leaders in Uganda." Social Science Information, Vol. XLVI, no. 2, pp. 53-78.

SATHYAMURTHY, T. V. (1966) Central-Local Relationship at the District Headquarters. Conference Papers (no. 380). Kampala: EAISR (mimeographed).

SCHNELL, R. (1957) Plantes alimentaires et vie agricole d'Afrique noire. Paris: Larousse.

SCOTT, R. (1966) The Development of Trade Unions in Uganda. Kampala: East African Publishing House.

SHILS, E. (1965) "Charisma, Order and Status." American Sociological Review, Vol. XXX, no. 2, pp. 199-213.

––– (1961) "Center and Periphery." The Logic of Personal Knowledge. London: Routledge and Kegan Paul, pp. 117-130.

––– (1960) "Political Development in the New States." World Politics, Vol. XII, pp. 329-368.

––– (1958) "The Concentration and Dispersion of Charisma: Their Bearing on Economic Policy in Underdeveloped Countries." World Politics, Vol. XI, No. 1, pp. 1-19.

SOUTHALL, A. W. (1963) Micropolitics in Uganda–Traditional and Modern Politics. Conference Papers (no. 163). Makerere: EAISR.

UGANDA, Government of (1960) 1959 Census. Entebbe: Government Printer.

UGANDA, Republic of (1969) Background to the Budget 1969-70. Entebbe: Ministry of Finance.

––– (1962) Five-Year Development Plan. Entebbe: Ministry of Planning and Economic Development.

––– (n.d.) Work for Progress, Uganda's Second Five-Year Plan 1966-71.

––– (n.d.) 1968 Statistical Abstract. Entebbe: Ministry of Planning and Economic Development.

VAIL, D. (1968) Group Farming and Statecraft in Uganda. Rural Development Research Papers (no. 71). Makerere: Economic Research Seminar (mimeographed).

WATTS, E. R. (1969) Staffing Aspects of the Extension Saturation Projects in Uganda. Rural Development Research Papers (no. 90). Makerere University College (mimeographed).

–––(1969) Agricultural Extension Services in Uganda. Uganda Agricultural Soc. Jour., Vol. II, No. 2.

–––(1968) Education Constraints on Peasant Agriculture. Rural Development Research Papers. Makerere University College (mimeographed).

WEINTRAUB, D. (1970) Traditions and Change, and Change and Traditions: Some Thoughts on Comparative Analysis of Symbolic and Institutional Aspects of Modernization. Paper submitted to the Seventh Congress of the European Society of Rural Sociology, Munster.

WELBOURN, F. B. (1965) *Religion and Politics in Uganda 1952-1962.* East African Publishing House.

YELD, R. (1965) Resettlement in its Effects on Kiga Patterns of Life. Makerere: Sociology 1.

BARUCH KIMMERLING was born in Rumania and immigrated to Israel in 1952. He obtained his B.A. in sociology and political science, in 1965 from The Hebrew University, and his M.A. from the same institution in 1968. Since 1969 he has been a scientific worker at the Department of Sociology at The Hebrew University where he is also teaching courses on sociology of conflict, social change in developing countries, sociology of the Israeli-Arab conflict and its influence on Israeli society, and social psychology.

MOSHE LISSAK is a native of Israel, and received his B.A., M.A. and Ph.D. degrees from The Hebrew University. In 1961-1962 he was a Fellow of the Committee for Comparative Study of New Nations at the University of Chicago, and in 1967-1968 he was a Research Fellow at the Center for International Affairs at Harvard University. In addition to his appointment as Senior Lecturer at The Hebrew University, he is editor of Magamot *(Behavioral Sciences Quarterly) and is a consultant to the Israeli Parliament on social issues.*